EART...

Traveling California's Fault Lines

D. Perkins, U.S.G.S.
MARINA DISTRICT, LOMA PRIETA QUAKE 10/17/89

A RENAISSANCE HOUSE PUBLICATION

ISBN: 1-55838-120-1

RENAISSANCE HOUSE
A Division of Jende-Hagan, Inc.
541 Oak Street ~ P.O. Box 177
Frederick, CO 80530

Cover Photo by D. Perkins, U.S. Geological Survey

10 9 8 7 6 5 4 3 2 1

WELCOME

In the days following the 1989 Loma Prieta earthquake, many California residents weighed the risks vs. the benefits of living on the Ring of Fire. Commented the *San Francisco Bay Guardian*: "We're gambling against fate, and last week our luck ran out. It was inevitable-- as the infamous bumper sticker says, 'Mother Nature bats last.'" Travelers to the land of faults and rifts must be as fatalistic as its residents; fatalistic but not pessimistic.

The National Earthquake Information Center in Golden, Colorado, which measures earthquakes around the world, locates 12,000-14,000 quakes each year-- roughly 35 per day. The center anticipates an average of 18 major earthquakes (7-7.9 on the Richter Scale) and one "great" quake (8+) annually. California can expect a 6.0 magnitude quake every two years, on average, and a 7+ earthquake every 10-15 years. But recently the number of major quakes has fallen short of the predicted average, indicating that earthquake frequency is not on the rise.

Most Californians try to believe the odds are in their favor. Distance from the epicenter helps tremendously. The strength of a quake is cut in half at a distance of 8 miles from the affected fault segment. At 17 miles, it's only 25 percent as strong. Likewise the duration of the quake diminishes the farther one is from the source. The most intense shaking during the Loma Prieta quake lasted only 10-15 seconds, while shaking in other large earthquakes has lasted as long as 30-40 seconds. The longer the shaking, the greater the damage.

This guide offers information about current seismic conditions in California, a history of past quakes, and a forecast of the future, based on reports from earth scientists. But there is much more to be learned. Some suggestions for further reading on California earthquakes:

  Earthquakes, B.A. Bolt
  Earthquake Country, R. Iacopi
  The Coming Quake, T.A. Heppenheimer
  Terra Non Firma, J.M. Gere & H.C. Shah
  California's Changing Landscapes, G.B. Oakeshott
  Peace of Mind in Earthquake Country, P. Yanev

In addition, many of the agencies listed on pages 46-48 offer free literature on earthquakes, faults, and emergency preparedness measures.

To answer the nagging question of why millions of Californians have chosen to live with their faults(!) consult these other fine guides in **The California Traveler** series:

Whale Watching & Tidepools   *   *California Missions*
 Parks & Monuments   *   *Gems & Minerals*

CONTENTS

Our thanks to Dr. Lind Gee at the Seismographic Station, Dept. of Geology and Geophysics, University of California at Berkeley, for her careful reading and consultation on the text.

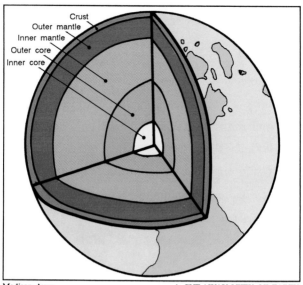

Madison Ayer
A CUT-AWAY VIEW OF EARTH

GEOLOGY OF EARTHQUAKES

Often in basic geology, the earth is compared to an apple. Just as an apple's center is its core, so is the earth's center its core. In fact, the earth has two cores-- a solid inner core and a liquid outer core. Beyond these cores are layers called the lower and upper mantle. The mantle is nearly 1800 miles thick, a dense region of rock which makes up a large part of the earth's mass. Outside the mantle layers is earth's thin crust-- comparable to the skin of the apple. The total distance from earth's surface to its inner core is nearly 4000 miles, while the crust is a mere 5 to 40 miles thick.

But in comparing earth with an apple, we must keep one major difference in mind. While an apple is static, the earth is not. The outermost layers of the earth (the crust and the top of the upper mantle) are broken into seven large, rigid plates as well as several smaller ones. These plates move about the surface of the earth, riding on the weak, partially molten layer below. The continents are imbedded in the plates and move passively with them. Although the movement seems small (only a few inches a year), it is tremendously potent. Most of the earthquakes recorded annually occur along plate boundaries.

What causes these plates to move? Most scientists believe that plate motion occurs in response to convection within the earth. Just as convection currents develop in a coffee cup, the internal heat within the

4

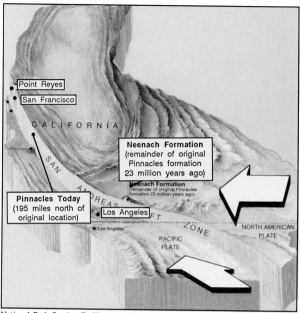

National Park Service, R. Hynes   PACIFIC AND NORTH AMERICAN PLATES

earth is redistributed by slow convection within the mantle. Hot material rises, is cooled, and sinks back into the mantle. The upwelling of hot mantle rock leads to the creation of new plate material along the oceanic ridge systems. At these places, the plates grow or spread apart, often in conjunction with volcanic and seismic activity. These "spreading centers", such as the mid-Atlantic ridge and the east-Pacific rise, are one of three types of plate boundaries.

While plates are created at spreading centers, they are destroyed in "subduction zones." At these convergent boundaries, the cold, dense oceanic plates are forced under the less dense continental plates. The trench systems of Japan and South America are examples of areas where oceanic plates are being overridden by the continental counterparts.

In the third type of plate boundary, plates slide past each other, neither creating nor destroying material. Of the many "transform" boundaries on the earth, the most famous is the San Andreas Fault.

Most of the earth's seismicity--its earthquake activity--occurs within narrow zones along plate boundaries. Plotting these points on a map delineates these tectonic margins. Particularly striking is the line of seismicity which runs along the western coast of North and South America, across the Aleutian Islands, and down through the Asian coastal waters. This pattern of earthquake activity, which correlates with active volcanoes, is known as the Ring of Fire.

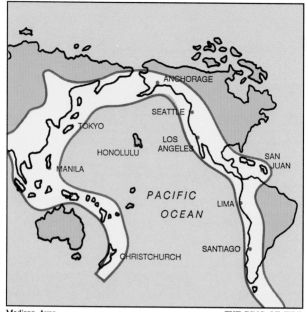

Madison Ayer

THE RING OF FIRE

Despite its location, California has suffered less earthquake damage thus far than many of its brethren around the Ring. Not only does the area have fewer large earthquakes, California's stringent building codes have helped prevent considerable property damage.

But even lesser seismic activity can create great destruction and chaos. The frightening aspect of California's location is its tremendous concentration of people. The potential for loss of life is enormous. So is the potential for damage. With the large populations come large apartment and office buildings, massive dams, nuclear reactors, and complex communications systems.

Every year, California experiences more than 10,000 earthquakes. Fortunately most of these are small in intensity and destructive potential. But at least one damaging quake occurs every year or two, and the potential for a severe quake is every 10 to 15 years.

Earthquakes can also occur underwater, within the ocean floor. Such quakes create huge movements of water once called tidal waves but now known as *tsunamis*, a Japanese word meaning "huge wave." A tsunami can travel as fast as 600 m.p.h., and although it may not appear overwhelming out in the middle of the ocean, it can be 50 feet high by the time it reaches shore. In Japan, where these underwater quakes occur with greater frequency than in many other parts of the world, tsunamis are dreaded events which have caused tremendous destruction and death.

University of Colorado   EARTH CRACKS NEAR EL CENTRO, 10/15/79

Why is California such prime earthquake country? Because it is the meeting point of two tectonic plates. The Pacific plate is moving northwest relative to its eastern neighbor, the North American plate. In California, this boundary takes the form of transform motion on the San Andreas Fault system. Along this major fault and many smaller ones branching from it, most of California's earthquakes have occurred.

Regardless of where an earthquake occurs, it is the result of energy being released inside the earth. This commonly occurs along faults, where two blocks of the earth's crust have become displaced in relation to one another. This displacement can be the result of horizontal movement, vertical movement, or both. The horizontal movement creates *strike-slip* faulting, while vertical movement makes *dip-slip* faulting. Faults typically move in accordance to one of these patterns, although many show both types of motion. It is along these faults--the weak spots in the earth's crust--that earthquakes occur with repeated frequency.

What happens is this: over time, various blocks of the earth move with respect to each other, primarily in response to plate tectonic motion. At first this movement is resisted by the strength of the rocks, causing stresses to build up within the blocks. When the stresses exceed this strength, the blocks will rupture (usually along existing planes of weakness such as faults) and slip to accommodate the required motion. Thus the elastic energy stored in the rocks by the slow deformation over tens or hundreds of years is released in seconds in the form of an earthquake. This theory of "elastic rebound" was first hypothesized after the destructive 1906 earthquake.

Portions of a fault may be "locked," meaning that they don't move significantly over a century or more.

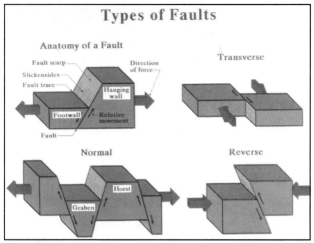

Types of Faults

Anatomy of a Fault

Fault scarp
Slickensides
Fault trace
Hanging wall
Footwall
Relative movement
Fault
Direction of force

Transverse

Normal

Horst
Graben

Reverse

National Geophysical Data Center   TYPES OF FAULTS

Other portions may "creep" by slipping slowly without creating an earthquake. Although the locked portions of the faults are quiet, the pressure beneath them continues to build. When it reaches the breaking point, the resulting quake is often of a larger magnitude than those in the creeping portions.

Scientists describe earthquakes by two reference points. One is the *focal depth*. This is the distance from the quake's point of origin in the crust or mantle up to the surface. The other is the *epicenter*, the point on the surface of the earth that is straight up from the focal point. From the focus of an earthquake, the vibrations radiate outward, getting weaker as they move farther away.

Most earthquakes occur in the earth's crust or upper mantle--relatively near the surface in comparison to the total radius of the earth. Quakes may occur near the surface, just a few feet into the crust layer, or down hundreds of miles. Those near the surface, not exceeding 38 miles deep, are considered shallow. Most quakes originate here, about 10 to 20 miles down. An intermediate quake is one with a focal depth from 38-188 miles. Deep quakes can reach levels of 440 miles underground.

When underground pressure causes the earth's crust to snap or "fault," an earthquake occurs. The vibrations that result from the earthquake are *seismic waves*. Sometimes small earthquakes called *foreshocks* precede the main quake. In the hours or days before a quake, there may be repeated small foreshocks. This subtle cracking of the earth's crust is a dark warning of what lies ahead.

Earthquake Eng. Res. Inst.   ROOF FAILURE, 6.7-M COALINGA, 5/2/83

Vibrations generated by an earthquake can be divided into two groups: body waves and surface waves. Body waves travel through or within the body of the earth and are of two types. The first are *compressional waves* that make a thud or shock when the earthquake strikes. They travel away from the epicenter at the rate of 3 to 7 miles per second, like sound waves travel through the air. Because they complete their travel first, they are called primary or "P" waves.

Following the P wave comes a rolling motion created by side-to-side movement through rock. This is the *shear wave*, a slower-moving wave which reaches the surface of the earth later than the P wave. Shear waves are known as secondary or "S" waves. Since S waves cannot pass through liquids, they do not penetrate the molten part of the earth's core.

The second type of waves are *surface waves*. These longer waves travel slower, along the earth's surface. Surface waves are the largest in an earthquake. They cause the most damage at the epicenter and can radiate shock several hundred miles away.

What is it like at the center of a damaging earthquake? One geologist said the tremor was "hard enough to stop a moving person." Shock waves often follow the main impact to produce a rolling motion on the ground's surface. Their strength builds quickly to the point that buildings start to collapse. In most cases the main event is over in less than four minutes.

U.S.G.S., G. Reagor   AFTERSHOCK EFFECTS, WHITTIER NARROWS 10/1/87

Left: bell tower cracked during main shock. Right: bell tower destroyed during large aftershock.

SELECTED RICHTER / MERCALLI READINGS

Earthquake	Richter	Mercalli
Los Angeles area 12/21/1812		X
San Francisco area 6/10/1836		X
San Francisco area 6/1838		X
Fort Tejon 1/9/1857		X - XI
Eureka 10/1/1865		VIII - IX
Santa Cruz Mts. 10/8/1865		VIII - IX
Hayward 10/21/1868		X
Owens Valley 3/26/1872		X - XI
San Francisco 4/18/1906	8.3	XI
West of Pt. Arguello 11/4/1927	7.5	IX - X
Long Beach 3/10/1933	6.3	IX
Imperial Valley 5/18/1940	7.1	X
Kern County 7/21/1952	7.7	X
San Fernando 2/9/1971	6.4	VIII - XI
Eureka (off shore) 11/8/1980	7.0	VII
Coalinga 5/2/1983	6.7	VIII
Loma Prieta 10/17/1989	7.0	IX

MEASURING EARTHQUAKES

The Greek word *seismos* meaning "shock" is the root of many words pertaining to earthquakes. A seismologist is a scientist who studies earthquakes, while a seismograph is an instrument for measuring the vibrations created by an earthquake. Seismographs have been set up all over the world to monitor quakes. These sensitive instruments magnify the movements of the ground beneath them, giving seismologists the data they need to pinpoint the location, magnitude, and origin of the earthquake. A seismogram is the zig-zag line produced by a seismograph which records the quake's vibrations.

There are several methods for measuring the size of an earthquake; the two most common are magnitude and intensity. Generally the magnitude reflects energy release, whereas intensity records ground shaking and damage. The more common measurement and the one most associated with earthquake reports is the Richter Magnitude Scale. This scale, developed by Dr. Charles F. Richter and his associates at the California Institute of Technology, is based on the measurement of the maximum amplitude on recorded seismograms. From this measurement, an estimate can be made of the amount of energy released.

The Richter Scale is logarithmic, so an earthquake of magnitude 7 produces a recording 10 times larger

A MEASURE OF DAMAGE, 6.8-M IMPERIAL VALLEY

than that of a magnitude 6. In terms of energy release, however, a magnitude 7 is 30 times greater. Earthquakes as small as magnitude .1 are routinely recorded in California, but earthquakes less than 2 are not perceptible to most people. Those greater than magnitude 5 are considered major earthquakes. There is no upper limit to the Richter Scale.

While magnitude provides a uniform measure of earthquake size, it does not accurately assess the amount of damage caused by an event. For measuring intensity of an earthquake, seismologists use the Modified Mercalli Scale, its readings being in Roman Numerals ranging from I to XII. A quake at the low end of the scale is not usually felt. A reading of XII reflects total destruction.

Measurements on the Mercalli scale require eyewitness reports of damage. Because the information gathered is based on the report of the observer and therefore subjective, the scale does have its limitations. Nevertheless, it remains one of the most practical methods of assessing the intensity of a quake, for the descriptions offered in each of its 12 ratings leave little room for doubt. For instance, the description of a VI quake reads approximately, "Felt by all, many frightened. Some heavy furniture moved; a few instances of fallen plaster. Damage slight."

Measurement on the Richter Scale allows one earthquake to be compared to another. The Mercalli rating is a more accurate assessment of damage. Thus a low Richter rating might get a high Mercalli rating, depending on the level of damage. And a high Richter quake occurring in a sparsely developed area would likely get a low Mercalli rating. The amount of destruction depends much more on local geologic conditions, the time of day the quake occurred, its duration, and the design of man-made structures in the area than it does on the magnitude of the quake.

STREAM OFFSET ALONG SAN ANDREAS FAULT

SAN ANDREAS FAULT SYSTEM

The San Andreas Fault is a long, narrow breach in the crust of the earth. For 15 to 20 million years it has been the location of periodic earthquakes, seemingly inconsequential until mankind began living along it. This fault, like most, is filled with crushed rock. At its narrowest point it is a few hundred feet across; at its widest, nearly a mile. It varies in depth, at some points extending 10 miles below the earth's surface.

The San Andreas, more than 800 miles long, comes on shore at Cape Mendocino north of San Francisco and extends south to the San Bernardino area. At Cajon Pass, the San Andreas branches into several smaller faults, among them the San Jacinto and Banning. Heading south the San Andreas then runs under the Gulf of California, for it is an extension of the rift that divides Baja from mainland Mexico.

You can see the fault in several places. It appears as a long trough and is particularly striking from the air. On the ground you may see streams take a quick jog off course, an indication that you are within fault boundaries. The presence of linear ridges and valleys, scarps (sharp, cliff-like landforms), and sag ponds (small lakes located in depressions at the foot of scarps), are all indicative of a fault zone. One of the most easily visible areas is on central California's Carrizo Plain.

In the case of the San Andreas (but not all faults), the fault line is the junction of two major tectonic plates. Here, a strip of the North American (continental) plate has actually become attached to the oceanic Pacific plate and is traveling northward with it. The southwestern slice of California along with Baja make

13

FENCE OFFSET BY FAULT IN MARIN CO., 1906

up this "attachment" to the Pacific plate. The plates drift, and the San Andreas accommodates this movement.

If you look across the fault you may see indications of movement along these plates. The portion across the line will seem to have moved to the right. In geologic terms this is a "right-lateral strike-slip" motion. If you can locate a road, fence, or other linear feature in the fault area that is older than the most recent seismic activity there, you may be able to see where the offset has taken place. In 1906, a maximum 21 feet of offset was observed; in 1989, 7 feet of horizontal slip was measured along a 25-mile segment of the San Andreas southwest of San Jose.

The tectonic plates on either side of the San Andreas drift one to two inches per year. Assuming the plates maintain this average over the next 10 to 20 million years, the movement will bring Los Angeles adjacent to San Francisco. Both earthquakes and fault creep are manifestations of this movement. Because the plates are sliding against one another, the movement is erratic and friction is created. Pressure builds until the friction is overcome and fault slip takes place. This release of pressure and the subsequent rebounding motion creates an earthquake which can travel along the fault as fast as a thousand miles per hour.

In the great span of time since the fault was born, it has shifted some 350 miles. Evidence of this is found near Tejon Pass where 150 miles now divides areas that were once adjacent; other blocks of the earth's crust

NEAR OLEMA IN MARIN CO., 1906

have shifted as much as 20 degrees in latitude.

Does movement along the fault *cause* the earthquake? Or are fault movements the *result* of an earthquake? For many years scientists argued this point. It was a study of the San Andreas Fault after the 1906 San Francisco earthquake that finally brought them to the conclusion that most earthquakes are caused by sudden movement along a fault.

Not all areas of the San Andreas Fault have a history of intense seismic activity. Those regions where there have been few earthquakes are called *seismic gaps*. Fault movement is not as frequent here, but that fact makes the region prone to large quakes as the pressure continues to build without intermittent releases.

Two areas of the fault which worry seismologists most are the San Francisco and LA portions, as these high population areas are also spots where the fault appears to be "locked"--no significant movement has occurred here since the major quakes of 1857 and 1906. Smaller quakes have occurred on side faults since then, but seismologists think such movement may actually increase the pressure on the San Andreas. So, say scientists, the question is not *if* the San Andreas will rupture again soon; only *when*.

Univ. of Colorado   FAULT TRACE, IMPERIAL VALLEY QUAKE 1979

OTHER MAJOR FAULTS

The San Andreas Fault does not bear the burden of California's tectonic pressure alone. In the San Francisco area are eight other sizeable faults, among them the Calaveras, Hayward, and San Joaquin. California earthquake activity in 1836 and 1868 was along the Hayward. Running NE/SW in the west central part of the state near Bishop is the Owens Valley Fault, which experienced considerable slip during the earthquake of 1872. North of Los Angeles on an E/W route is the Garlock Fault. Just east of where the Garlock bisects the San Andreas, considerable fault creep occurs.

Near San Bernardino the San Andreas branches south. Two of its major branches are the San Jacinto and the Banning Faults. The former has seen much earthquake activity in the last hundred years, beginning in the 1890's with quakes in the Anza and San Bernardino Valley regions. In 1918 a quake hit the San Jacinto Valley along this fault, and in 1968 nearby Borrego Mountain.

In the southeastern corner of the state a third fault, the Imperial, joins the system. This fault was first identified during a quake on May 18, 1940. In October 1979 another one struck, confirming that the Imperial is part of the San Andreas system. These secondary faults can help to relieve pressure, somewhat reducing the severe earthquake potential that exists elsewhere along the San Andreas.

U.S.G.S., G. Reagor   PARKING GARAGE, 5.9-M WHITTIER NARROWS 10/1/87

PAST CALIFORNIA QUAKES

Every year California experiences thousands of small earthquakes. Each is a clue to weak spots or faults in the earth's crust. Although the San Francisco earthquake of 1906 has received much attention historically, a number of other quakes have struck the state in the past 200 years, some of them equal to the 1906 event.

Santa Barbara, Ventura and LA Counties, 1812

Earthquake damage to public buildings in early 19th century California meant missions. On December 8, 1812, about 7 a.m., a quake destroyed or severely damaged several such structures. A foreshock about one-half hour before the main event probably saved many lives.

Just two weeks later, on December 21, about 11 a.m., another quake hit, this one just off the coast. Aftershocks of substantial strength continued into February of 1813 and lesser ones were felt into April. Although data is incomplete, it appears that this quake may have triggered a tsunami. Interestingly, the New Madrid earthquakes were occurring in Missouri about the same time, 1811-1812.

San Francisco Bay, 1836; San Francisco, 1838

Near San Francisco runs the Hayward Fault, a 40-mile rift which parallels the San Andreas 18 miles to the east. Here a sizeable quake struck on June 10, 1836, creating aftershocks which would last a month. Just two years later, in June of 1838, a quake again hit the San Francisco region, this time along the San

BAREPP   6.3-M WESTMORLAND QUAKE, 4/26/81 (Note undamaged structure on left)

Andreas Fault, shortly after noon. Scientists say its shock was comparable to the one which struck San Francisco in 1906, but without the large numbers of people and buildings to suffer damage, it did not make a place in history as the later quake would.

Fort Tejon, 1857

The quake of 1857 was southern California's strongest in historic times. It struck about 8 a.m. on January 9 with more than three minutes of ground shaking. The earth ripped apart along the San Andreas Fault for 217 miles through the central part of southern California. Because the state was sparsely settled at this time, there were few horrifying tales of collapsing buildings or massive death. In fact only two deaths were reported. At Fort Tejon, an army post 60 miles north of Los Angeles, the base commander watched as his entire post collapsed.

The 1857 quake's epicenter was near where the Garlock Fault meets the San Andreas. Movement was very similar to that in San Francisco in 1906--right lateral strike-slip motion. Scientists who studied the displacement of stream beds recorded as much as 29 feet of movement. Although devices and systems for recording the magnitudes of earthquakes were not in place at this time, data indicates that the '57 quake was of about the same intensity as the 1906 quake in San Francisco.

Since 1857, no significant quake has occurred along this stretch of the San Andreas, leading scientists to predict that southern California is overdue for a major earthquake. History bears out this prediction. Since the

18

TWISTED PORCH COLUMNS, COALINGA, 5/2/83

6th century, nine major earthquakes have struck in the area of the 1857 quake, averaging about 160 years between upheavals.

Northern California, 1865

On October 1, about 9:15 a.m., a quake of sizeable intensity (VIII-IX) struck near Eureka and Fort Humboldt. All of the buildings were damaged and huge redwoods uprooted. Just one week later, on October 8 at 12:46 p.m., another earthquake of like intensity hit the Santa Cruz Mountains. Greatest damage was done in the stretch from San Jose to Santa Cruz. Great clouds of dust were given off as the earth opened and closed in different places.

Hayward, 1868

Along the same fault that fractured in 1836, activity again occurred on October 21, 1868. Although the earlier events had been of equal or greater intensity, greater destruction occurred in 1868, for the area was now more populated. Nearly every building in Hayward suffered extreme damage and San Francisco's losses exceeded $350,000. Thirty people were reported dead. Aftershocks continued into November.

Geologists believe the 1865 Santa Cruz quake and the 1868 Hayward event may have been part of the paired earthquake theory, wherein one quake acts as the precursor of another a few years later. But the paired earthquake theory may be no more than chance. Scientists just aren't sure.

U.S.G.S.   5.9-M LIVERMORE EARTHQUAKE, 1/24/80

Owens Valley, 1872

Near the tiny town of Lone Pine, along today's Hwy. 395 just west of Death Valley, disaster struck on March 26. An earthquake of a X-XI Mercalli reading, felt strongly over 125,000 square miles, struck the area about 2:30 a.m. The force of the quake was probably felt over much of Nevada and Arizona as well as California. On March 17 a smaller quake was recorded at Lone Pine, and on March 23 another near Austin in central Nevada. These tremors may have presaged the jolt which hit Owens Valley. The tremors resulted in 23 feet of vertical displacement and 20 feet of horizontal displacement along the fault.

The quake of March 26 caused 27 deaths and 56 injuries just in Lone Pine; in all, 60 people died. Many adobe houses were destroyed. Thousands of aftershocks followed the quake, some of them severe. The National Oceanic and Atmospheric Administration rated the Owens Valley shock "greater than those of 1857 and 1906."

San Francisco, 1906

One of the greatest seismic events ever to strike California began at 5:12 a.m. on April 18, 1906, just west of the Golden Gate of San Francisco. But it was felt over a 375,000 sq. mi. area, from Oregon to Nevada, and would register on seismographs around the world.

The 1906 quake occurred along the San Andreas Fault, creating the largest known length of slip along a fault plane in the lower 48 states. In all, the fault ruptured over a distance of 270 miles in a northwesterly direction. The greatest single segment of slip was in Marin County, where the fault moved 21 feet.

U.S.G.S., G.K. Gilbert   BUCKLED RAILWAY TRACKS, SAN FRANCISCO, 1906

Seismologists think the rupture initiated off the Golden Gate and emanated north and south. It roared onto the mainland at a velocity of 7000 m.p.h., ripping a path with a force greater than all the explosives used in World War II. Before it was over, the great San Francisco earthquake would register a Mercalli intensity of XI, a record which would not be set again until the Kern County quake of 1952.

Destruction covered a 400-mile area. Huge redwoods and thousands of smaller trees were uprooted. Roads buckled and pipelines burst, sewer lines were destroyed, and streetcar tracks were twisted and torn. Some of the greatest destruction occurred where broken water mains disabled San Francisco's fire department. Gas mains, too, were broken, adding unwanted fuel to the raging fires. More than four miles of downtown San Francisco was quickly reduced to rubble.

In Santa Rosa, 19 miles from the fault, damage was also severe. The reason, seismologists say, is that it lay straight east from the point of greatest slip on the San Andreas. Some 50 deaths were recorded here. In the western San Joaquin Valley, 30 miles from the fault, the Mercalli rating reached IX.

Some strange, quake-related phenomena also occurred in the water. In San Francisco Bay the tide began to drop until it was down four inches. Water apparently drained out through the Golden Gate into the Pacific Ocean, then congregated again and rushed back into the Bay, flooding spots along shore.

HOWARD ST. NEAR 17th, SAN FRANCISCO, 1906

Aftershocks continued to pound the city, one strong enough to cause landslides on April 25, and the last large one recorded in July. Of the 700 people ultimately lost, 315 died and 352 were never found. More than 28,000 buildings were destroyed. When citizens began rebuilding, they dumped earthquake rubble into San Francisco Bay. The new buildings constructed on this base of unstable landfill will, seismologists say, now be the most vulnerable in a future quake.

The quake caused $400-million worth of damage by 1906 standards; $1.6-billion by today's. Considering the city's development, a similar sized earthquake today would cause $40-billion in damage. Population increases would put the death toll in the tens of thousands.

Long Beach, 1933

Fire caused more damage than the earthquake itself in San Francisco; the opposite was true in Long Beach in 1933. Although the Long Beach quake was of average magnitude, damages of $40 million were reported. Poor building construction made this quake one of the most destructive in U.S. history.

The 1933 earthquake occurred along the Newport-Inglewood Fault, which had been discovered just 13 years earlier and named for the towns on its landward extremities. The quake's epicenter was just offshore

BAREPP   6.2-M MORGAN HILL QUAKE, 4/24/84

near the pier in Huntington Beach, its force shattering
the southern part of the fault.

About 120 people perished in the Long Beach
quake. The toll would have been much higher had
school been in session, for schools with their brick and
mortar construction were some of the most vulnerable
buildings. Within two months of the quake, state
legislators had passed the Field Act, applying severe
engineering codes to school construction, in an effort to
make schools as earthquake-proof as possible. The Act
worked well in new schools, but there was no provision
for bringing older buildings up to standard until 1967.
Many scientists say that a future quake along the
Newport-Inglewood Fault would be at least 1-1/2 times
as devastating as the largest one forecast on the San
Andreas.

Imperial Valley, 1940

The farthest south that a major earthquake has hit
California was in the Imperial Valley on May 18, 1940.
The epicenter was just southeast of El Centro, affecting
a 60,000-square-mile area. Irrigation systems in this
highly agricultural region were devastated. Damage
was reported at $6-million, not including loss of crops,
and with only nine fatalities.

By magnitude, this quake was not quite as strong as
the Kern County quake. The rupture changed the
Mexican/American border by jogging the International
Canal nearly 15 feet. Because of this quake, scientists

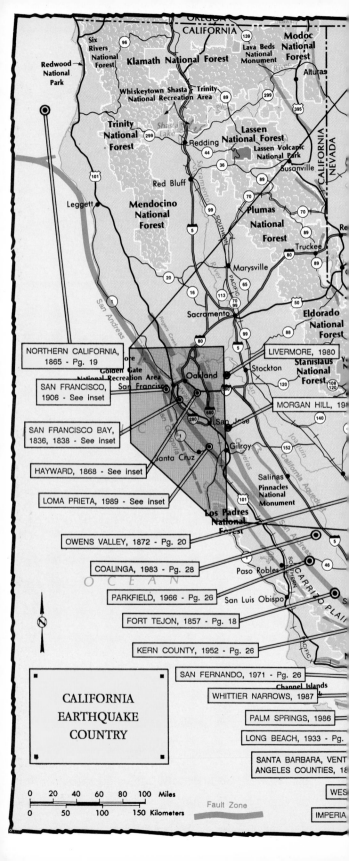

NORTHERN CALIFORNIA,
1865 - Pg. 19

SAN FRANCISCO,
1906 - See inset

SAN FRANCISCO BAY,
1836, 1838 - See inset

HAYWARD, 1868 - See inset

LOMA PRIETA, 1989 - See inset

OWENS VALLEY, 1872 - Pg. 20

COALINGA, 1983 - Pg. 28

PARKFIELD, 1966 - Pg. 26

FORT TEJON, 1857 - Pg. 18

KERN COUNTY, 1952 - Pg. 26

SAN FERNANDO, 1971 - Pg. 26

WHITTIER NARROWS, 1987

PALM SPRINGS, 1986

LONG BEACH, 1933 - Pg.

SANTA BARBARA, VENT
ANGELES COUNTIES, 18

WES

IMPERIA

LIVERMORE, 1980

MORGAN HILL, 19

CALIFORNIA
EARTHQUAKE
COUNTRY

| 0 | 20 | 40 | 60 | 80 | 100 | Miles |
| 0 | 50 | 100 | | 150 | Kilometers |

Fault Zone

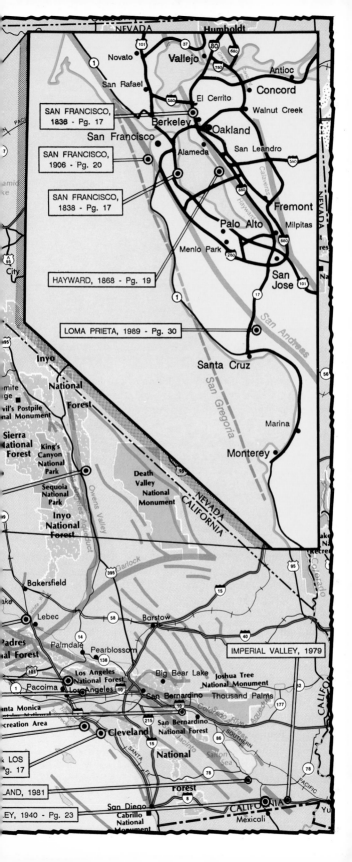

NEVADA
Humboldt

101
Novato
37
80 680
Vallejo
780
San Rafael
Antioc
El Cerrito
580
Concord
Walnut Creek

SAN FRANCISCO,
1836 - Pg. 17
Berkeley
Oakland
San Francisco
San Leandro

SAN FRANCISCO,
1906 - Pg. 20
Alameda
580
880
Calaveras

SAN FRANCISCO,
1838 - Pg. 17
Hayward
Fremont
Milpitas

Palo Alto
680

HAYWARD, 1868 - Pg. 19
Menlo Park
280
San Jose
101

17
Na

LOMA PRIETA, 1989 - Pg. 30
San Andreas

Santa Cruz
56

395
Inyo

National
San Gregoria

Marina

mite
ge
Forest

vil's Postpile
al Monument

Sierra
ational
Forest
King's
Canyon
National
Park

Monterey

NEVADA
CALIFORNIA

Sequoia
National
Park

Owens Valley

Death
Valley
National
Monument

Inyo
National
Forest

ake
Na
Recre

Colorado

99

95

395
Garlock

Bakersfield

15

Lebec
58
Barstow

14
40

adres
al Forest

Palmdale
Pearblossom

IMPERIAL VALLEY, 1979

101
138

1
Pacoima
Los Angeles
National Forest
Big Bear Lake
Joshua Tree
National Monument

Los Angeles
10
Thousand Palms

nta Monica
ical Na
creation Area
San Bernardino

10
177

215
San Bernardino
National Forest
86

Cleveland
15
SOUTHERN
Salton
Sea

78

National

78

LOS
g. 17
Forest
8

AND, 1981

EY, 1940 - Pg. 23
San Diego
CALIFORNIA
Yu

Cabrillo
National
Monument
Mexicali

U.S.G.S., G.K. Gilbert   BLUXOM ST. & 6th, SAN FRANCISCO, 1906

were able to locate the exact line of the Imperial Fault, which had not previously been identified. Not far from the 1940 site, another magnitude 6.7 earthquake struck in October 1979.

Kern County, 1952

Nearly 100 years later and about 30 miles northeast of Fort Tejon, another quake occurred not far from the region of the 1857 quake. This was the Kern County quake of 1952, centered on the White Wolf Fault at a point south of Bakersfield. The Kern County event was the largest earthquake in the U.S. since the San Francisco quake of 1906. Property damage was nearly $50-million, but only 12 people died. The quake struck on July 21 with aftershocks--an amazing 180 of substantial magnitude--continuing through September 26. Smaller ones were recorded for years.

Parkfield, 1966

During the last century a medium-range (6.0) quake has occurred about every 20 years near Parkfield, California, the most recent in 1966. This regularity makes it the most predictable stretch of fault in the world, so predictable that government scientists gather here with sensitive recording instruments to learn more about what precipitates an earthquake.

San Fernando, 1971

In comparison to the quakes of 1906 or 1857, the San Fernando tremor of 1971 was mild, only 1/500th as strong in terms of energy released. More than 800

MORGAN HILL, CALAVERAS FAULT, 4/24/84

homes were destroyed, 64 people died, and the area suffered a half billion dollars in damage. Yet this was considered only a moderate quake.

Some of the greatest damage in the San Fernando event was to roadways, $20- million in destruction to the freeway system and another $5-million in smaller roads. Because the quake struck at 6:00 a.m., the loss of life was much less than it might have been during a heavy commuting period.

Five dams were severely damaged by the quake, but again providence was on the side of the locals. The water level was below normal that February 9, so when a huge portion of one dam collapsed, the reservoir into which it fell was not overtopped. Another bit of providence was that the main quake lasted only 60 seconds. Had there been further sizeable tremors, one or more of the other dams might have collapsed, threatening 80,000 residents in the immediate area.

The town of Sylmar was hardest hit. The next day's *Los Angeles Times* said it looked as if "a huge hand had reached down, picked up the entire community, and given it a terrible shaking." Busy intersections appeared to have been plowed up as if for planting. Scientists speculate that two sets of S-waves may have struck here, causing this intense upheaval.

Perhaps the most significant aspect of the San Fernando quake, however, was its value as an object lesson in unpreparedness. Californians--Los Angeles

U.S.G.S., M. Hopper   2ND STORY WALL COLLAPSES, COALINGA, 5/2/83

area residents in particular--saw how woefully inadequate their emergency procedures were for the Big Quake. Local fire and police agencies were slow to respond. The collapse of an entire wing of a hospital went unreported for 1-1/2 hours after the quake. Communications systems were rendered inoperative when power failed and there were no backup sources. Few communities had emergency operations centers where civic leaders could converge to direct rescue and clean-up programs. There was concern from the Hispanic community that too few Spanish-speaking civil defense workers were available, resulting in a misunderstanding of directions and procedures. There were complaints that the streets remained crowded with impassable clutter for up to two weeks after the event.

The 1971 quake occurred on a small fault. But after studying and analyzing the 1971 tremor, the Los Angeles Earthquake Commission released a map showing 42 different faults which bisected the metro area. Developers and real estate people condemned the map as inflammatory and misleading, but the overall threat to residents became strikingly clear.

Coalinga, 1983

When, on May 2, 1983, an earthquake struck Coalinga in central California, scientists were not even aware of the fault which produced it. It was an unmapped fault which seismologists had yet to identify. Yet in the space of seconds this quake of moderate magnitude along an unknown fault had caused $33-million in damage. No deaths were reported, but 164 people were injured, 16 of them seriously. More than 800 homes were severely damaged, with most of the

PORCH FAILURE, COALINGA, 5/2/83

damage occurring in the downtown Coalinga area. Tremors were felt from Los Angeles to Sacramento and from San Francisco to Reno, Nevada.

The scientifically intriguing aspect of the Coalinga quake is the presence of a major *fold* in the area. Folds in this region appear on the surface as hills and depressions. The epicenter of this 1983 quake was beneath a hilly rise called the Coalinga Anticline. Scientists say the quake occurred on a *thrust* or *reverse fault,* along an inclined plane deep underground.

Instead of two plates moving against each other in opposite directions, as with earthquakes along the San Andreas Fault, the movement in this quake was upward along the thrust fault. The unnerving aspect to scientists-- for it creates the likelihood of surprise quakes--was that this upheaval never broke the surface of the earth. The only way to tell the location of these thrust faults was by the folds created on top of them. Identifying the Coalinga fold prompted scientists to investigate other California folds, for now they realized their potential as future quake sites.

The Coalinga quake renewed ongoing research in the area of earthquake prediction. A Japanese seismologist, Kiyoo Mogi, had, in the late 1960's, identified what became known as Mogi's Doughnut. In China, Mogi had tracked a pattern of moderate sized quakes which occurred in a ring around an area of quiet. As Mogi predicted, a stronger quake shortly occurred within this center of calm.

In 1975, a similar pattern began to emerge in the Coalinga area. Over the next seven years, three more

quakes completed the perimeter of the ring. In the center, things were quiet--until May 3, 1983, when the Coalinga earthquake filled in the doughnut's hole. Still, although Coalinga might have been identified as a potential trouble spot because of its plotting on the "doughnut graph," there was still no warning in the form of foreshocks. Even if scientists are able someday to pinpoint *where* earthquakes will occur, it will do people little good unless they know *when*.

Loma Prieta, 1989

Figures of seismic activity along the San Andreas Fault show some noticeably quiet areas. These are called seismic gaps--sections of little or no movement along the fault. Because of the inactivity, pressure builds along these segments, making them the most vulnerable to large quakes. In one of these seismic gaps, near a point where the San Andreas Fault changes direction from north to west, the Loma Prieta earthquake of 1989 occurred.

During this quake, the North American and Pacific plates were only doing what they have done for millions of years: moving. In this case the Pacific plate moved northwest 6.2 feet which caused it to travel up and over the North American plate 4.3 feet. Seismologists say that the upward motion is related to the curve that the San Andreas Fault takes east of Santa Cruz.

The Loma Prieta quake took place along one of six sections of California faults that seismologists had deemed most likely to suffer a major shock between 1988 and 2018. But 30 years is a wide span of time in

FAILED SECTION S.F.-OAKLAND BAY BRIDGE

which to pinpoint a seconds-long event. Yet the Loma Prieta experience aided scientists' forecasting capabilities for future quakes.

Although the quake occurred in the Santa Cruz Mountains, the major damage was in the San Francisco and Oakland areas, some 50 miles away. One of the most heavily damaged sections was the Marina District. During the 1906 earthquake this area was a lagoon. Detritus dumped into the Bay after that quake provided the landfill for today's Marina District. Because of this unstable landfill, the ground during the Loma Prieta event actually became liquefied. Damaged gas and water mains gave firefighters the same nightmares they had in 1906. Although structural quality had improved greatly since then, there was still a lack of lateral bracing on multi-storied buildings.

The Loma Prieta earthquake occurred on October 17, 1989, at 5:04 p.m., heavy drive time. The failure of highway structures took a heavy toll and gave the earthquake its notoriety. The upper level of the Nimitz Freeway, I-880, collapsed onto the lower road, crushing 41 motorists. The ultimate death toll of 67 was small compared to other events of its magnitude. Just ten months earlier a comparable sized earthquake in Armenia took 25,000 lives. Improvements in construction and community preparedness contributed to the lower loss of life. Dollar damage was substantial, however: $7-billion. Within three weeks after the quake, 4,760 aftershocks had been recorded, 20 of them strong, and two caused further damage. Another 65 were substantial enough to be felt by area residents.

EFFECTS OF WEAK FIRST STORY, LOMA PRIETA

ANTICIPATING & PREVENTING EARTHQUAKE DAMAGE

It doesn't take a Richter or Mercalli scale to answer everyone's basic question regarding earthquake damage: 'How bad was it?' The answer is measured in two ways: loss of property and loss of life. How many were killed and how many dollars worth of damage was done? Loss of life and property is the ultimate measure of any earthquake damage.

Ineffective design of buildings and highways is a major culprit in damage to both life and property. In 1973, many California communities adopted a strict Uniform Building Code. Structures built since that date pose fewer hazards than older ones. Among the most vulnerable types of buildings are unreinforced masonry, where walls are not fastened securely to floor or roof. The "tilt-up" design is also earthquake vulnerable, for buildings tend to fail where the sections of concrete meet. Another culprit is the concrete frame structure common in commercial and office buildings before 1976. Not only are these buildings less sound structurally, they have the potential for greater loss of life, since they were designed to house large numbers of workers.

Other types of buildings subject to earthquake damage are those designed with weak first stories, such as apartment complexes with parking garages on the

RESULT OF LIQUEFACTION, LOMA PRIETA

ground level. As evidenced in the Loma Prieta earthquake, when the columns supporting these garages give way, the whole building can collapse.

The geology of an area is a critical factor in determining earthquake vulnerability. Ground near a fault is often unstable and less competent to withstand the shock of a quake. Steep slopes where land has slid or settled in the past are likely to do so again. Much of the inland portion of the San Francisco Bay Area is composed of this unstable bedrock.

The coastal Bay region is composed primarily of mud and fill, strongly prone to liquefaction during a quake. The probability of ground failure in such areas is very high. Just inland from the shoreline around the three major bays is an area of unconsolidated soil, very likely to shake in a tremor, particularly when wet. Land that has liquefied in one quake is highly likely to perform the same way during subsequent tremors.

This unstable ground base combined with the presence of the San Gregorio, San Andreas, Hayward, Calaveras, Concord, Green Valley, and Rodgers Creek Faults--all in the San Jose, San Francisco, Santa Rosa stretch--make this extremely vulnerable earthquake territory. Earthquake-wise residents are advised to have buildings they frequent assessed for structural security. Government agencies such as those on p. 48 can supply geologic maps and reports regarding ground stability for most regions of California.

BAREPP   6.0-M PALM SPRINGS QUAKE, 7/8/86

PERSONAL PREPAREDNESS

REMEMBER: the greatest danger in an earthquake is not from the shaking ground. It is the potential collapse of surrounding structures or fixtures. Quake area dwellers are well-advised to familiarize themselves with the local emergency procedures regarding earthquakes. Within the home, most veterans of fault zones keep an emergency kit prepared in a basement or windowless area and in the car. The kits should contain a change of warm clothing, a reliable radio, a flashlight with extra batteries, a fire extinguisher, first aid supplies, non-perishable food, and one gallon of water per person per day. Families as well as communities should have a plan of action for earthquake situations.

During the earthquake, keep away from windows, chimneys, and large, tall pieces of furniture. In an office, get under a desk or in an interior doorway. It is usually better to stay indoors, but if you must leave a public building, do not rush for the exit. If driving, the safest place is in the car, parked in an open area away from bridges and overpasses.

Civil defense experts agree: the best precautionary measure against earthquake damage is to understand the hazards. Damaging earthquakes will occur in our lifetime in California. Travelers and residents alike should identify and study the potential sites and structures most likely to affect them.

U.S.G.S., D. Perkins   AFTER LOMA PRIETA, 10/17/89

THE BIG ONE: WHEN? WHERE?

It's not a matter of "if." In 1988, the National Earthquake Prediction Evaluation Council said there was a 50% probability for an earthquake of magnitude 7.0 or larger within the San Francisco Bay Area in 30 years or less. It estimated a 30% likelihood for a 6.5 to 7.0 quake in the Santa Cruz Mountains. The Loma Prieta earthquake, a 7.1 magnitude tremor, had its epicenter in the Santa Cruz Mountains.

But Loma Prieta was not the "big" one. In July 1990, the U.S. Geological Survey said, "There is a 67% chance of another earthquake the size of Loma Prieta" in the Bay Area before the year 2020. Such an earthquake could strike at any time, the study said. The U.S.G.S. suggested that the next Bay Area quake might strike farther north than did Loma Prieta, between San Jose and Santa Rosa, in a more densely populated area, giving it the potential for greater destruction.

Seismologists rely heavily on data from past quakes to understand the future. But still the science of prediction remains inexact. In the 70 years preceding the San Francisco quake of 1906, there were six earthquakes of magnitude 6.5 or greater in the Bay area. But in the 85 years since, only two such sized quakes have occurred. Scientists conclude that the 1906 tremor released pressure in the earth which allowed it to be relatively quiet until 1979. But since that year, there have been four major quakes of 6.0 or greater, leading some seismologists to think that the earth is preparing for another major happening.

Scientists can point a finger at fault locations that have slipped in the past, with reasonable assurance that they will be tomorrow's culprits. The larger the quake, the larger the segment of fault that will be affected. Likewise, accumulated strain along a particular section is a sign that that segment may be preparing to slip again. So it was that in 1981, seismologists recognized that a major earthquake on the Santa Cruz section of the San Andreas fault was likely to occur before 1996. They were right.

The San Andreas is not alone. The National Earthquake Prediction Council has pinpointed three other segments likely to cause large quakes in the Bay Area over the next 30 years: the Hayward Fault between Fremont and San Leandro and from there to San Pablo Bay; and the Rodgers Creek Fault between San Pablo Bay and Santa Rosa. There may be more than one 7.0 quake or larger during this time which, because of greater population density, could be more destructive than the Loma Prieta event.

Nor may the occurrence be isolated to one fault; seismologists have noted a recurring pattern of paired earthquakes. For example, the VIII-IX intensity quake of 1865 on the San Andreas was followed three years later by a IX-X intensity quake on the Hayward. Such examples cause scientists concern that the Loma Prieta quake may be the first of such a pair.

And What of Southern California?

Seismologists say that a quake of 7.5 or larger on the San Andreas Fault is <u>more</u> likely in southern than in northern California. For the past 200 years in southern California, says the U.S.G.S., "an earthquake of magnitude 6.5 or greater has occurred along the San Andreas and related faults every 10-20 years." The sections of the fault most likely to breach in the next event are the Coachella Valley and San Bernardino Mountains segments between Los Angeles and the Mexican border; and the Mojave and Carrizo segments north of LA toward San Luis Obispo. Along the San Jacinto Fault, which runs west of the San Andreas south of LA, seismologists say the Anza portion has a 30% probability of a magnitude 7.0 quake by the year 2018. The Imperial Fault near the Mexican border has a 50% chance of a 6.5 quake by the same year.

But the area where scientists are now focusing their attention and prediction tools is the Parkfield area of the San Andreas. This segment, just north of San Luis Obispo, has a *greater than 90% probability of a magnitude 6.0 earthquake by 1993*. This section of the fault--known as the most predictable in the world--

breaches about every 22 years, the last occurrence being in 1966 of a 5.3 magnitude.

Earthquakes in California are inevitable. Through increasingly reliable data and sophisticated technology, scientists can now forecast earthquakes in certain areas. But accurate prediction is still a dream of the future.

Seismologists expected the Loma Prieta quake. For several years they had been watching the Loma Prieta, San Francisco, and Parkfield sections of the San Andreas Fault. They knew that because there had been little recent activity in these areas, that pressure would soon reach a breaking point. On June 27, 1988, a magnitude 5.0 struck near the Santa Cruz Mountains. On August 8, 1989, a 5.2 quake occurred in nearly the same area.

Knowing that approximately half of California's major earthquakes have had such foreshocks less than five days before the main event, the California Office of Emergency Services put out public advisories warning residents of an increase in seismic risk. Scientists had been right in their prediction, but wrong on the time. The anticipated quake did occur--not five days but two months after the last foreshock. The areas that suffered the greatest devastation during the Loma Prieta quake had been targeted some 15 years earlier as being geologically hazardous. Unfortunately it was not possible to predict when those hazards would manifest themselves.

Data from each successive event provides seismologists with a clearer picture of the earthquake rupture

BAREPP   EFFECTS OF LIQUEFACTION, MORGAN HILL 4/24/84

process. In the past 30 years, more than a dozen major earthquakes world-wide have been predicted with reasonable accuracy. Unfortunately some of the best techniques for prediction are developed by studying quakes while they are occurring--something of a Catch-22 situation.

Seismographs throughout the world record earthquake activity. Seismologists use these recordings to study the rupture process of earthquakes, in hope of predicting them some day. Small tremors are not necessarily precursors of large earthquakes and major quakes are not always preceded by foreshocks. In addition to variations in seismicity, geologists and geophysicists study phenomena such as changes in water and gas pressure, changes in electro-magnetic properties, and changes in local ground deformation.

A University of California geologist noted unusual flows of oil prior to a 1925 quake in the Santa Barbara area. After the foreshock but before the main quake, oil began oozing onto the beach. Such seepage was noted again prior to small quakes in 1969 and '70. Similarly, scientists at the National Oceanic and Atmospheric Center in Boulder, say that changes in the patterns of geyser eruptions can help predict earthquakes near the geysers. Many scientists are studying fault movements, measuring pressure buildup, monitoring smaller shocks and the tilting or shifting of the earth's crust in an effort to forecast earthquakes.

Ken Waller   THOUSAND PALMS OASIS

TRAVELING THE FAULTS

Where can travelers go to visit earthquake country?
A number of sites are marked with reminders of
destruction from past quakes, although the rubble has
long since been cleared. Some of these spots now house
earthquake monitoring equipment accessible to the
public. In other areas, travelers can stand on faults or
view evidence of them nearby.

In Southern California:

To see a rare positive effect of fault movement,
head south into the palm deserts. There, near the oases
that provide life-giving water to the palm trees, will be
a fault. The fault has trapped underground water which
provides the supply for these oases. One of the most
spectacular examples of the palms' symbiosis with a
fault is on the San Andreas at **Thousand Palms Oasis**,
near the town of that name in Riverside County.

The San Andreas and San Jacinto Faults run
through **San Bernardino National Forest**. One or the
other of these faults produce tremors in the forest
almost daily, but few are noticeable to travelers. Near
the faults is Big Bear Lake dam which would almost
certainly fail during a major quake, flooding a large
portion of the national forest and creating a severe
hazard to travelers. The San Andreas runs across the
national forest from Cajon Pass, southeast along the
San Bernardino Mountains to Banning Pass.

Located in the **Angeles National Forest** (headquartered in Arcadia) is the **Pacoima Fault,** near the community of the same name. There are several faults in this area, but the Pacoima is the easiest to spot. Although it is not listed on major fault maps, its location directly northeast of the densely populated San Fernando Valley, makes it of interest.

Thousands of years of earthquake upheaval can be seen at **Devil's Punchbowl,** a park administered by Los Angeles County and located in Pearblossom, within the Angeles National Forest. Giant weathered slabs of conglomerate rock project upward in all directions from this geologically intriguing cup-shaped park. At the visitor center, travelers can find explanations of the geologic activity and the faults that run through the area, among them the San Andreas. Also within the national forest is the **Hamilton Preserve,** a wildlife sanctuary whose landscape was created by two currently active faults. On the north is the San Andreas and to the south is the San Jacinto.

Palmdale, just south of Lancaster, is another good San Andreas viewing spot. Along Hwy. 14, in a rock cut made during road construction, travelers can see evidence of great tectonic upheaval in the geologic formations, caused by movement of the San Andreas.

Along the **Los Angeles Aqueduct Bikeway** is evidence of geologic wonders that have been formed by the San Andreas Fault. The section of this 107-mile bike path that is best for seeing the fault is in Antelope Valley, which can be accessed from either the Quail Lake or Silverwood Lake terminus.

Fort Tejon State Historic Park near Lebec was the site of disastrous earthquake damage in 1857. The

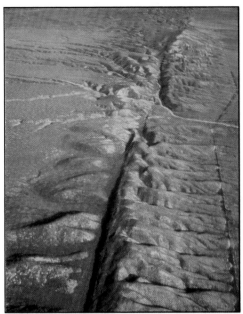

SAN ANDREAS FAULT NEAR CARRIZO PLAIN

adobe army post was badly damaged. Today, three earthquake monitoring stations in the park record activity along the faults that pass through this area.

The San Andreas Fault runs some 800 miles within California, from the Mexican border to Point Arena in Mendocino County. One of the best places for viewing or standing on it is the **Carrizo Plain** in southeastern San Luis Obispo County. The plain is about 50 miles long by 6 miles wide, a tract of arid, uninhabited land. To access the Carrizo Plain, travel to Kern County via Hwy. 166/33 or Hwy. 58. The Soda Lake region is a good area from which to view the fault.

A traveler looking across the San Andreas can see that ground on the opposite side appears to have moved to the right. This is the "right lateral slip" characteristic for which the San Andreas is known. Certain streams in this area have been offset by fault slippage as much as 30 feet or more and can be identified because they make a sharp turn just after crossing the fault line. Other fault-related features of interest are the straight, low cliffs called "scarps" which appear to have been eroded, but actually are the result of vertical movement along a fault. Another apparent feature are sag ponds, dips in the earth created by nearby fault upheaval which fill with water in a storm or can trap water like the oases mentioned earlier.

In Northern California:

The **Santa Cruz** area was the scene of much havoc during the 1989 Loma Prieta earthquake. Most of Pacific Garden Mall, located along Pacific Avenue, was destroyed in the tremor and three shoppers were killed. Travelers wishing to stand above the epicenter of the Loma Prieta quake should travel a short distance east to **Forest of Nisene Marks State Park**. At the end of a two-mile trail--specifically latitude 37 deg. 2 min.; longitude 121 deg. 53 min.--travelers will be standing at the point of origin. A 150-foot landslide and uprooted redwoods remain as reminders of the '89 devastation.

The epicenter was just five miles south and east of the **Loma Prieta School,** located in the Santa Cruz Mountains near Hwy. 17. Although the site has since been condemned for rebuilding, evidence of earthquake damage abounds here. There are benches, offset streams or drainage areas, and even an historic one-room school which still stands, but shows evidence of fault movement.

In the hills above Palo Alto is the **Los Trancos Open Space Preserve.** A hiking trail leads travelers along a half-mile, self-guided tour of the the San Andreas, locating sag ponds, scarps, and benches--areas of level land with steep slopes above and below, formed by nearby fault activity. The U.S.G.S. gives this area a 40% chance of a magnitude 6.5 quake in the next quarter century.

The **San Andreas Lake** and **Crystal Springs Reservoir**, located along the San Andreas Rift Zone on the San Francisco peninsula, are dammed by two structures which, amazingly, survived the 1906 earthquake. This rift region is an interesting one for seismologists, because it marks a boundary on the San Andreas. North of here, the 1906 quake caused much greater offsetting than it did farther south. This, say seismologists, could mean that a major earthquake will occur sooner on the southern portion than on the northern.

About 10 miles southeast, in the city of **Fremont,** is Central Park, an area that that sits higher than the land around it for it has been pushed up from each side by two traces of the Hayward Fault. At the peak of this elevated park is perched the Fremont City Hall.

Running along the Hayward Fault through Fremont is a section of pipeline that has been moved above ground to protect it from movement. This pipeline, which supplies water to San Francisco, has been bent by fault creep despite its above-ground placement.

The Hayward branch of the San Andreas offers travelers further visible evidence of earthquake activity. The Hayward runs from San Pablo Bay to Mount Misery, east of San Jose, a stretch of metropolitan area that is home to more than a million people. In the city

BERKELEY STADIUM, ON THE FAULT

of **Hayward**, travelers can see the result of fault creep between A and D Streets, from Mission Blvd. to Main. Curbs are offset, sidewalks have repaired fault cracks, and buildings show long cracks in their walls.

Another public facility which is at the mercy of the Hayward Fault is **Fairmont Hospital** in San Leandro. The fault extends along a low hill behind the hospital and runs beneath some of the buildings at the facility.

Dams and highways in proximity to the fault are in danger of fracturing should the Hayward breach. Hwy. 24 in **Oakland**'s Montclair District is one example. The idea to elevate a section of this road where it intersects Hwy. 13 was vetoed due to earthquake concern. In fact, the valley through which Hwy. 13 runs was created by constant movement of the fault. Nearby is Lake Temescal, actually a sag pond, formed by thousands of years of movement of the Hayward Fault. A dam, constructed to take advantage of this natural pond, sits precariously near if not *on* the fault.

Certain buildings at the **University of California at Berkeley** are also vulnerable, where the Hayward Fault runs along the campus' east side. Walls are separating in the university's Memorial Stadium which sits directly on the fault. Strawberry Creek that runs under the stadium has been offset by as much as 1/4 mile due to earthquakes and fault creep in the area. A corner of Bowles Residence Hall may also may sit directly on the fault. The university is taking steps to make certain facilities are more seismically sound. The campus's Earth Sciences Building has an exhibit on earthquakes

43

Mission San Juan Bautista   MISSION SITS ON THE SAN ANDREAS FAULT

and seismograms as well as a display seismograph.

To view the epicenter of the 1906 earthquake, stand on the Golden Gate Bridge and look west toward Mussel Rock. Just south of the bridge lies Daly City, a modern metropolis built right on top of the fault. Building took place prior to zoning regulations which would have prevented such a hazardous location. Daly City was the epicenter of the quake which struck in 1957.

Evidence of the 1906 earthquake can still be seen in some parts of **San Francisco.** Travelers should head for an alley between 5th and 6th streets, south of Mission, actually on Tehama Street. Here are some vintage warehouses whose condition speaks for the seismic force that once struck--and will strike again--in the San Francisco Bay area. The San Francisco City Museum also has displays and photographs documenting both the 1906 and 1989 earthquakes.

Coastal Hwy. 1 in many places parallels the San Andreas Fault, running east of it between **Olema** and the **Bolinas Lagoon.** Travelers turning off Hwy. 1 onto the Drake Hwy. near Point Reyes Station, cross from one tectonic plate onto another: from the North American to the Pacific Plate. In this area of heavy tectonic activity, one can see sag ponds and low ridges, both the result of movement along the fault. Actually there are many faults in proximity here. To see what natural confusion they have caused, note that Olema Creek and Pine Gulch Creek--although running very near each other--actually flow in opposite directions. The Olema Valley Trail, a 5.2-mile hike, runs along the San Andreas from Five Brooks to Dogtown.

DRAKES BAY, POINT REYES NAT. SEASHORE

The San Andreas Fault makes itself known at several points in the northern part of the state before it heads out to sea at Cape Mendocino. At **Point Reyes National Seashore**, travelers can take a half-mile walking tour of the area affected by the 1906 quake. Man-made straight-line features, such as fences and highways, help the traveler see the effects of tectonic activity, where offsetting has occurred due to fault movement. Such is the case here with the Sir Francis Drake Hwy. which was offset 15-20 feet during the 1906 event. The tour also passes a large barn on the Skinner Ranch which sits directly atop the fault.

Evidence of long-term seismic activity--perhaps 20 million years--is offered by **Mt. Wittenberg**, another site along the Point Reyes earthquake trail. This mass of granite once lived 350 miles to the south near Bakersfield, on the other side of the San Andreas. Millenia of slippage and upheaval moved the massif to its current location.

* * * * * * * * * * * * * * * * * * *

Despite the geologic odds against them, Californians are pragmatic about the danger of their location. Said one public official after the Loma Prieta quake, "We [realize] we'll never be a match for Mother Nature."

U.S.G.S., G. Reagor   DRUG STORE SHELVES, IMPERIAL VALLEY 10/15/79

INFORMATION CENTERS

Many government agencies are involved in the monitoring, reporting, and studying of earthquakes. The **United States Geological Survey** offers services and literature through a variety of its departments. Among its services is the **Earthquake Hotline**, updated daily. For a report call: (415) 329-4025.

The U.S.G.S. also encompasses the **Earth Sciences Information Centers**, of which there are three in California. They conduct research, compile data, answer questions, and issue publications with the latest seismic information.

In Los Angeles:
7638 Federal Bldg., 300 North Los Angeles St. (90012) (213) 894-2850.

In Menlo Park:
345 Middlefield Rd. (94025); (415) 329-4390

In San Francisco:
555 Battery St., Room 504 Custom House (94111) (415) 705-1010

The National Earthquake Information Center, another division of the U.S.G.S., is located in Golden, Colorado. This agency is the foremost collector of rapid earthquake information in the world and has the responsibilities for the Earthquake Early Alerting Service (EEAS). This 24-hour service requires the NEIC to determine the location and magnitude of significant earthquakes around the world and convey this information to government agencies responsible for emergency response. More than 3000 stations report to the NEIC; 100 of

U.S.G.S., G. Reagor   WALL COLLAPSE IN ALHAMBRA, 10/1/87

them are part of the U.S. Seismic Network and their data is recorded in Golden. The NEIC also publishes reports and information of interest to the public, such as *Earthquakes and Volcanoes*, a bimonthly publication of the U.S.G.S., oriented toward the layman.

National Earthquake Information Center
PO Box 25046 DFC, MS-967; Denver, CO 80225
(303) 236-1510

At the state level is the **California Division of Mines and Geology**, which develops Earthquake Planning Scenarios, and publishes maps and reports. The agency's monthly publication is "California Geology" which describes earth science issues for the layman.

California Division of Mines and Geology
PO Box 2980; Sacramento, CA 95812-2980
(916) 445-5716

Two other state offices of seismic importance are:

California Office of Emergency Services
2800 Meadowview Rd., Sacramento CA 95832
(916) 427-6659.

Among this office's excellent publications are two called "Living on the Fault." One details sites on the Hayward Fault; the other sites on the San Andreas.

The California Seismic Safety Commission
1900 K St., Suite 100, Sacramento CA 95814-4186
(916) 356-6329

Issues construction guidelines for earthquake zones.

There are three regional government offices of earthquake study and preparedness in the state which distribute free literature and other information on earthquake preparedness measures:

IMPERIAL CO. SERVICES BLDG., 10/15/79

ABOVE: *Before (left) and after (right) pictures from the Imperial Valley quake show how the support columns failed, threatening the collapse of the structure.*

Bay Area Regional Earthquake Preparedness Project (BAREPP)
Metro Center, 101 8th St., Suite 152
Oakland, CA 94607; (510) 893-0818

Southern California Earthquake Preparedness Project (SCEPP)
1110 East Green St., Suite 300
Pasadena, CA 91106; (818) 795-9055

Southern California Earthquake Preparedness Project (SCEPP)
1350 Front St, Suite 4015
San Diego, CA 92101; (619) 238-3321

The **American Red Cross** publishes several inexpensive handbooks on Earthquake and Disaster Preparedness:

American Red Cross, Contract Educational Services
2700 Wilshire Blvd; Los Angeles CA 90057
(213) 739-5293

An Annotated Bibliography for Urban and Regional Planners Interested in Reducing Earthquake Hazards, along with a monthly newsletter is available from:

Earthquake Engineering Research Institute
6431 Fairmount Ave., Suite 7
El Cerrito, CA 94530-3624; (510) 525-3668

The **National Geophysical Data Center** and the **National Oceanic and Atmospheric Administration** are concerned with management of data pertaining to the atmosphere, space, land, sea, and Earth's interior. A catalog of services is available:

325 Broadway, Boulder, CO 80303; (303) 497-6215